12 QUESTIONS ABOUT THE
US CONSTITUTION

by Kate Conley

www.12StoryLibrary.com

12-Story Library is an imprint of Peterson Publishing Company and Press Room Editions.
Produced for 12-Story Library by Red Line Editorial

Photographs ©: www.BillionPhotos.com/Shutterstock Images, cover, 1; AS400 DB/Bettmann/Corbis, 4, 7; Jack E. Boucher/Library of Congress, 5; AP Images, 6, 12; John F. Weir/Library of Congress, 8; Augustus Tholey/Library of Congress, 10, 28; Pendleton's Lithography/Library of Congress, 11; StockPhotosLV/Shutterstock Images, 14; Everett Historical/Shutterstock Images, 15; Orhan Cam/Shutterstock Images, 16; Evan Vucci/AP Images, 18; US Army, 19; Cameron Whitman/Shutterstock Images, 21, 29; Harris & Ewing/Library of Congress, 22; Elias Goldensky/Library of Congress, 23; Bettmann/Corbis, 25, 27; King & Baird/Library of Congress, 26

Library of Congress Cataloging-in-Publication Data
Names: Conley, Kate A., 1977- author.
Title: 12 questions about the US Constitution / by Kate Conley.
Other titles: Twelve questions about the United States Constitution
Description: Mankato, MN : 12-Story Library, 2017. | Series: Examining
   primary sources | Includes bibliographical references and index.
Identifiers: LCCN 2016002346 (print) | LCCN 2016002596 (ebook) | ISBN
   9781632352897 (library bound : alk. paper) | ISBN 9781632353399 (pbk. :
   alk. paper) | ISBN 9781621434566 (hosted ebook)
Subjects: LCSH: United States. Constitution | Constitutional history--United
   States. | Constitutional law--United States.
Classification: LCC KF4541 .C555 2016 (print) | LCC KF4541 (ebook) | DDC
   342.7302--dc23
LC record available at http://lccn.loc.gov/2016002346

Printed in the United States of America
Mankato, MN
May, 2016

Access free, up-to-date content on this topic plus a full digital version of this book. Scan the QR code on page 31 or use your school's login at 12StoryLibrary.com.

Table of Contents

What Is the US Constitution? 4

Why Was the US Constitution Written? 6

What Happened at the Constitutional Convention? 8

Who Wrote the US Constitution? 10

How Was the US Constitution Ratified? 12

How Is the US Constitution Organized? 14

What Is the Legislative Branch? 16

What Is the Executive Branch? 18

What Is the Judicial Branch? 20

Can the US Constitution Be Changed? 22

What Is the Bill of Rights? 24

Is the US Constitution Useful Today? 26

Fact Sheet 28

Glossary 30

For More Information 31

Index 32

About the Author 32

What Is the US Constitution?

In May 1787, a group of men met in Philadelphia, Pennsylvania. The United States had won its freedom from England just four years earlier. With this freedom came many challenges. One of the biggest was setting up a federal government. Important steps were taken at the Constitutional Convention.

The country's new government needed to be powerful enough to unite the 13 states. It could not be too powerful, however. It needed

GO TO THE SOURCE

To read the full text of the US Constitution, go to **www.12StoryLibrary.com/primary**.

to allow states the freedom to govern themselves, too. It was a delicate balance. The leaders spent the summer discussing how it should work.

The product of their work was the Constitution. It was and still is the backbone of

George Washington presides over the Constitutional Convention.

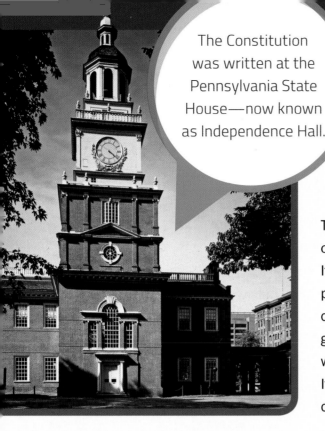

The Constitution was written at the Pennsylvania State House—now known as Independence Hall.

The people had no choice. The Constitution outlined a different plan. Every four years, Americans could vote to choose their leader.

The Constitution was unlike any other government plan at the time. It gave its citizens power and rights protected by the law. It also gave citizens a clear plan for how the government would be run. They knew what to expect from their leaders. It was an exciting idea for a new country.

the plan for the US government. The Constitution gives power to the president, Congress, and the Supreme Court. It also outlines which powers belong to the states and which belong to the federal government. These were new ideas at the time. In the past, most countries gave all their power to one ruler, such as a king.

The Constitution also gave American citizens the right to elect their leaders. This, too, was a new idea. Typically, leaders came from royal families. A king's child would automatically become the next ruler.

4
Number of months it took the delegates in Philadelphia to write the US Constitution.

- The Constitutional Convention began on May 25, 1787.
- The Constitution divides power between the president, Congress, and the Supreme Court.
- It also ensures that American citizens have the right to elect their leaders.

Why Was the US Constitution Written?

The US Constitution was written to replace the Articles of Confederation. The Articles had been adopted in 1777. They were the nation's first plan for government. The Articles made each colony an independent state. They also united all the states together as one nation.

But the union was a loose one. The states held most of the power. The federal government had little control. Some states began acting as if they were their own countries. They began printing their own money. They even created treaties with other nations.

The Congress of the Confederation ran the federal government. It could

A R T I C L E S
OF
CONFEDERATION AND PERPETUAL UNION,
BETWEEN THE STATES OF

NEW-HAMPSHIRE,
MASSACHUSETTS-BAY,
RHODE-ISLAND,
CONNECTICUT,
NEW-YORK,
NEW-JERSEY,
PENNSYLVANIA,

MARYLAND,
VIRGINIA,
NORTH-CAROLINA,
SOUTH-CAROLINA, AND
GEORGIA.

THINK ABOUT IT

Under the Articles of Confederation, Congress had a lot of power. Read Articles II and III of the Constitution. What are some ways that the power of Congress changed? Why do you think that was important to the founders of the United States? How might the US government look today if these changes had not been made?

The Constitution replaced the Articles of Confederation.

declare war, solve border problems, and make treaties. Congress did not have the power to tax its citizens. When it made requests of the states, some states often chose to ignore them. As a result, the government was often broke and powerless.

Leaders knew the government needed to be improved. Congress called for a convention in 1787 to revise the Articles. The delegates

8

Number of years that the Articles of Confederation served as the plan for the US government (1781–1789).

- The Articles joined all the states together loosely as a nation.
- The Congress of the Confederation could not tax its citizens.
- Passing laws and changing the Articles were slow, difficult processes.

to the convention realized the problems with the Articles were too great to fix. Instead, they decided to start over with a new document. It became the Constitution.

What Happened at the Constitutional Convention?

The Constitutional Convention was a meeting in 1787. American leaders gathered in Philadelphia to revise the Articles of Confederation. Fifty-five delegates were chosen by the states to attend the convention.

The delegates met in secret. Guards stood by the doors. Heavy curtains covered the windows. No reporters or visitors were allowed inside during the meetings. This let the delegates speak their minds without fear of others being able to influence them.

Instead of revising the Articles, the delegates decided to start over. First, they created the legislative branch of the government. It was led by Congress. Members of Congress would vote to make decisions that impacted the country. But the delegates disagreed about how to organize Congress. States with small populations wanted each state to have one representative in Congress. States with large populations disliked this plan. They believed the states with more people deserved more representatives.

Roger Sherman, a delegate from Connecticut, created a compromise. In Sherman's plan, Congress would have two equal bodies. The House

Sherman was given credit for the Connecticut Compromise, which created two equal bodies in the legislative branch.

THE DELEGATES

The delegates to the Constitutional Convention were an experienced group of leaders. Eight of them had signed the Declaration of Independence. Twenty-five had served in the Continental Congress. Fifteen of the delegates had helped draft constitutions for their home states. The men were also well-educated. Thirty-five of them were either lawyers or had undergone some type of legal training. The best-known delegate, George Washington, went on to become the nation's first president.

of Representatives would be based on population. The larger a state's population, the more representation it would have. In the Senate, each state would be represented by two people. In this way, both the small and large states would be represented fairly. This pleased both sides. It became known as the Connecticut Compromise.

The delegates then created the executive branch, headed by the president, and the judicial branch, led by the Supreme Court. The delegates also created a system of checks and balances. This prevented any one branch from becoming too powerful.

12

Number of states that sent delegates to the Constitutional Convention. Only Rhode Island did not send any delegates.

- The convention was held in secret so delegates could speak freely.
- The delegates compromised to make representation in Congress fair to both large and small states.
- Checks and balances stop one branch of government from becoming too powerful.

9

Who Wrote the US Constitution?

Records from the Constitutional Convention do not identify who wrote the US Constitution. Instead, most historians credit all 55 delegates as the writers. The group discussed and refined each idea before agreeing to it. Once they agreed on the basic ideas, the delegates appointed a committee to write them down.

Five delegates made up the Committee of Detail. They wrote the first draft. On August 6, 1787, they presented their draft. For the next month, all the delegates revised it.

The Committee of Style wrote the next draft. This group was made of five delegates. One of those delegates was Gouverneur Morris of Pennsylvania. Morris wrote the Constitution's introduction. It is called the preamble. Much of the

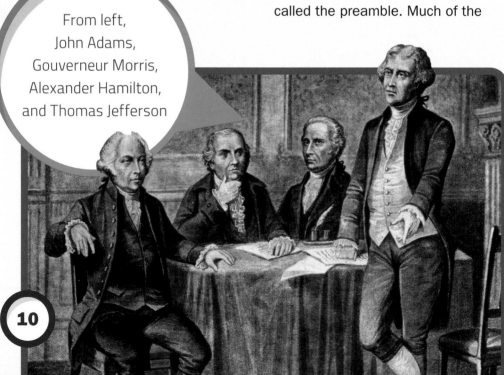

From left, John Adams, Gouverneur Morris, Alexander Hamilton, and Thomas Jefferson

4,543

Number of words in the final draft of the Constitution, including the signatures.

- The delegates wrote the Constitution as a group.
- Madison's detailed notes are some of the only records of how the Constitution was written.
- Committees wrote drafts of the Constitution, and the delegates revised the language.

Madison's detailed notes from the delegates' discussions helped him write sections of the Constitution.

wording in the Constitution is also credited to Morris.

James Madison was another Committee of Style delegate. Madison had helped organize the Convention. He proposed many ideas, such as voting by population. Madison kept detailed notes about the discussions and debates. He used them to write sections of the Constitution. For his work, he is often called the Father of the Constitution.

JACOB SHALLUS

Once the delegates had agreed to the wording, they needed a person to write the final document. They hired Jacob Shallus as the penman. He used a quill, ink, and four large sheets of parchment to write the final copy of the US Constitution. He had just two days to write more than 4,000 words in a neat, elegant script.

How Was the US Constitution Ratified?

On September 17, 1787, 39 delegates signed the US Constitution. But the process was not done. According to Article VII of the Constitution, 9 of the 13 states needed to ratify the Constitution. Then, it could take effect.

The people who wanted to approve the Constitution were called Federalists. They believed in a strong federal government. They believed that without it, the states would not be closely united. The new country might fall apart.

The Anti-Federalists opposed the Constitution. They believed it created a federal government that was too powerful. Anti-Federalists feared it would take too much power from the states and ignore citizens' rights. They demanded that individual rights be guaranteed in the Constitution before they would ratify it. Their concerns were

The delegates meet to sign the Constitution.

addressed by the addition of the Bill of Rights.

The debate in the country continued for months. On June 21, 1788, New Hampshire ratified the Constitution. It was the ninth state to do so. That made the Constitution the law of the land. Four states, however, had not yet signed it. The new nation was still in danger of falling apart.

Federalists worked to change the minds of people in the remaining

2

Number of years the Federalists spent trying to convince the citizens of Virginia, New York, North Carolina, and Rhode Island to ratify the Constitution.

- Citizens of the United States were divided about whether or not to approve the Constitution.
- Federalists believed in a powerful federal government.
- Anti-Federalists wanted a guarantee that individual rights would be protected.

THE FEDERALIST PAPERS

Three of the leading Federalists were Alexander Hamilton, James Madison, and John Jay. They worked to change public opinion about the Constitution. They did this by writing newspaper articles. Between 1787 and 1788, the men wrote 85 articles about the importance of ratifying the Constitution. These articles were published in papers across the country. They became known as The Federalist Papers. They played a large part in helping to ratify the Constitution.

four states. Their efforts were successful. Though the votes were close, the other states began to ratify the Constitution. On May 29, 1790, Rhode Island became the final state to ratify it.

How Is the US Constitution Organized?

The US Constitution is organized into three parts. The first part is the preamble. It introduces the ideas that will be presented in the Constitution. It promises the American people that their new government will strive for justice, peace, liberty, welfare, and defense.

The second part of the Constitution is a list of articles. The first three establish the branches of government. Article I creates the legislative branch. This branch makes laws for the country. Article II establishes the executive branch, which gives power to the president. Article III sets up the judicial branch. This branch is a system of federal courts.

The preamble to the Constitution explains that the government will provide for the defense of its people.

VOTES FOR WOMEN PROCESSION
LAFAYETTE SQUARE TO CAPITOL

The Constitution then turns its attention to other matters. Article IV divides powers between the state and federal governments. Article V outlines how changes can be made to the Constitution. Article VI makes the Constitution the highest law in the country. The last article explains what must happen to ratify the Constitution.

The last part of the Constitution is a list of amendments. They are changes to the document. The founders wanted to make sure the Constitution remained a useful document as the country grew. The amendments allow this to happen. The Constitution has been amended 27 times since it was written.

One of the 27 amendments to the Constitution gave women the right to vote.

7

Articles in the original Constitution.

- The Constitution is divided into the preamble, the articles, and the amendments.
- The articles establish the three branches of government.
- The amendments are changes made to the Constitution.

What Is the Legislative Branch?

Article I of the Constitution creates the US Congress. Congress makes federal laws for the country. It can also declare war, raise an army, tax citizens, and oversee trade. These powers belong only to Congress.

The Constitution divides Congress into two groups. One group is the House of Representatives.

The other group is the Senate. Together, they form the legislative branch of the government.

The Constitution establishes rules for each part of Congress. In the House, the number of representatives each state has is based on its

Both the Senate and House of Representatives meet at the US Capitol in Washington, DC.

MAKING LAWS

Every law Congress passes begins as a bill. Bills are ideas for new laws. Article I of the Constitution explains the process. If a bill is approved in the House of Representatives, it then goes to the Senate. Senators take their own vote, and if the bill passes there, it can then go to the president. The president has 10 days to sign a bill into law or veto it. Thousands of bills are proposed in one session of Congress. Of those, only about 5 percent actually become laws.

population. Large states have more representatives than small states. Voters elect their representatives every two years.

The Constitution sets up the Senate differently. Each state has two senators. It does not matter how large the state's population is. Each state is equally represented in the Senate. Senators are elected by the public. They serve six-year terms.

According to Article I, the House and Senate must meet at least once each year. For Congress to create a law, both the House and Senate must pass it. It then goes to the president, who can approve the law or veto it. This makes sure each law is carefully considered by a large number of people before taking effect. It is an example of checks and balances.

535
Number of members of the US Congress in 2016.

- According to the Constitution, Congress is divided into two houses, the Senate and the House of Representatives.
- The number of representatives each state gets in the House is based on population.
- Each state sends two senators to the Senate, regardless of population.

What Is the Executive Branch?

Article II of the Constitution creates the office of the president. The president leads the executive branch, which puts into effect the laws Congress has passed. To do this, the president works with 15 government departments. The Constitution allows the president to choose the department leaders. They are called the Cabinet.

The president works closely with Congress. After a law passes through Congress, the president signs it into effect. If the president disagrees with a law, he or she can veto it. If Congress disagrees with a veto, it can vote to override the veto. This is an example of checks and balances in the Constitution.

The Constitution gives the president other roles, too. The president can make treaties and name justices to the Supreme Court. The president is also

President Barack Obama (center) meets with his Cabinet in 2015.

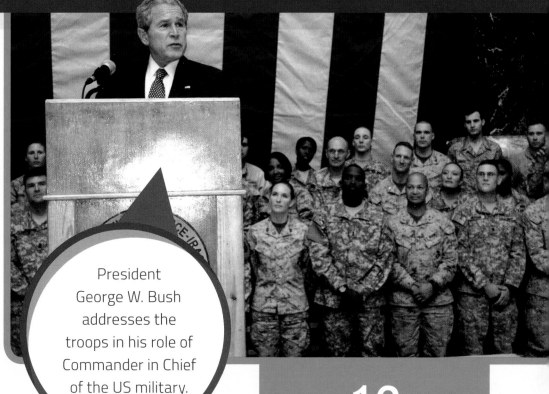

President George W. Bush addresses the troops in his role of Commander in Chief of the US military.

the Commander in Chief of the military. This means that if Congress declares war, the president has the final say on how the war is carried out.

Just as the Constitution describes the president's job, it also describes who can hold the office. The president must be a US citizen who has lived in the United States for at least 14 years. In addition, a president must be at least 35 years old. A person can be elected to two four-year terms as president.

12

Number of years Franklin Delano Roosevelt served as president before term limits were established.

- The Constitution names the president as the head of the executive branch of government.
- The president works with a Cabinet to make sure the government runs according to the law.
- The Constitution describes who is eligible to become president.

What Is the Judicial Branch?

Article III of the Constitution creates the Supreme Court. It forms the judicial branch of the US government. Its job is to interpret laws for the nation. The people who run the court are called justices. They decide which cases the court will hear.

The Constitution gives Congress power to create lower courts.

Congress has created 94 district courts and 13 courts of appeal. These courts hear cases that involve federal laws. Cases from the lower courts that are appealed can go to the Supreme Court for a final ruling. Because the Supreme Court is the highest in the land, its decisions are final.

Unlike the president or leaders in Congress, justices are not elected

9
Number of justices serving on the Supreme Court.

- The Constitution makes the Supreme Court the head of the judicial branch.
- Justices of the Supreme Court interpret the law in federal cases.
- Once a justice is appointed to the Supreme Court, he or she may hold that job for life.

THINK ABOUT IT

The Constitution lists specific requirements to become a president, representative, or senator. Read Articles I and II and find these requirements. The Constitution does not list any requirements for justices of the Supreme Court. What are some possible reasons the writers of the Constitution chose not to include any requirements for the justices?

The US Supreme Court Building is located in Washington, DC.

by the people. The Constitution gives the president the power to appoint justices. Then, the justices must be approved by the Senate. This is another example of checks and balances. If a justice is approved, he or she can have the job for life.

The Constitution also protects the legal rights of US citizens. The Fourth, Fifth, and Sixth Amendments provide guidelines on how a citizen can be treated under the law. A citizen is guaranteed a fair and speedy trial and the right to a

JUSTICE COUNT

The Constitution does not require a specific number of justices to make up the Supreme Court. Instead, that decision is left to Congress. Early in the country's history, that number changed often. The smallest Court had only five justices. The largest Court had 10. The Judiciary Act of 1869 set the number of justices at nine. It has remained unchanged since.

lawyer. Citizens are also protected from cruel or unusual punishments. They also cannot be tried twice for the same crime.

Can the US Constitution Be Changed?

The writers of the Constitution knew it was not a perfect document. They also knew their country was young. They thought it would grow and change. To make sure the Constitution would continue to serve the nation effectively, they wrote Article V. It allows changes to the Constitution. These changes are called amendments.

Though they wanted the Constitution to be flexible, the writers did not want it to change too much or too quickly. Article V describes the steps required for amending the document. It is a long, slow process. It requires the approval of many different groups.

Any amendment must first be proposed by two-thirds of Congress. Once an amendment has passed in Congress, it goes to the states. Three-quarters of the states must ratify the amendment by its citizens voting to approve it. Once this happens, the amendment is added to the Constitution.

More than 11,000 proposed amendments appeared in Congress between 1789 and 2014. Of that number, only 27 have been

Sixty-fifth Congress of the United States of America;

At the Second Session,

Begun and held at the City of Washington on Monday, the third day of December, one thousand nine hundred and seventeen.

JOINT RESOLUTION

Proposing an amendment to the Constitution of the United States.

Resolved by the Senate and House of Representatives of the United States of America in Congress assembled (two-thirds of each House concurring therein), That the following amendment to the Constitution be, and hereby is, proposed to the States, to become valid as a part of the Constitution when ratified by the legislatures of the several States as provided by the Constitution:

"ARTICLE —.

"SECTION 1. After one year from the ratification of this article the manufacture, sale, or transportation of intoxicating liquors within the importation thereof into, or the exportation thereof from the all territory subject to the jurisdiction thereof for beverage prohibited.

"S   ngress and the several States shall hav
to enfo   y appropriate legislation.
"   le shall be inoperative unless it sha
as an a   e Constitution by the legislatures o
as provid   Constitution, within seven years fro
submission hereof to the States by the Congress."

The 18th Amendment, adopted in 1920, prohibited the production and sale of alcoholic beverages in the United States.

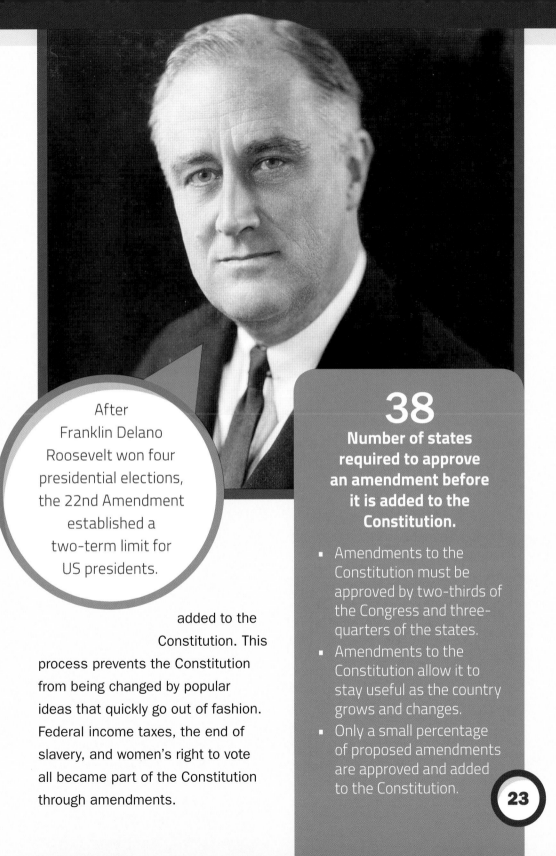

After Franklin Delano Roosevelt won four presidential elections, the 22nd Amendment established a two-term limit for US presidents.

38

Number of states required to approve an amendment before it is added to the Constitution.

- Amendments to the Constitution must be approved by two-thirds of the Congress and three-quarters of the states.
- Amendments to the Constitution allow it to stay useful as the country grows and changes.
- Only a small percentage of proposed amendments are approved and added to the Constitution.

added to the Constitution. This process prevents the Constitution from being changed by popular ideas that quickly go out of fashion. Federal income taxes, the end of slavery, and women's right to vote all became part of the Constitution through amendments.

What Is the Bill of Rights?

The first 10 amendments to the Constitution are called the Bill of Rights. They guarantee the rights of US citizens. Some of these are the right to freedom of speech and religion, the right to a speedy trial, and the right to bear arms.

The Constitution did not originally include a bill of rights. The delegates at the Constitutional Convention voted unanimously not to include one. They believed it was unnecessary. Most states already had their own bill of rights.

This decision was unpopular with the states. Americans remembered what it was like to be ruled by a

14

Number of copies of the Bill of Rights that were originally penned: one for each of the 13 states and one for the federal government.

- The writers of the Constitution believed that the federal government did not need a bill of rights because most states had their own.
- The promise of adding a bill of rights to the Constitution convinced the holdout states to ratify the Constitution.
- Many Americans wanted a bill of rights in the Constitution to protect their rights from a powerful government.

THINK ABOUT IT

Read the Bill of Rights closely. If it had not been added to the Constitution, in what ways might the country be different today? How would your daily life be different without these rights?

strong king with harsh laws. They did not want to lose their new freedoms. Americans wanted their new government to guarantee their rights. As a result, several states refused to ratify the Constitution without a bill of rights.

The states finally agreed to ratify the Constitution as long as a bill of rights would be adopted quickly. On December 15, 1791, the Bill of Rights was added to the Constitution. Today, the Bill of Rights continues to shape American values of freedom.

Protestors in 1964 rally to protect their freedom of speech, one of the personal freedoms guaranteed by the Bill of Rights.

Is the US Constitution Useful Today?

Although the US Constitution was written more than 200 years ago, it remains the very foundation of our country's government. Whenever Congress passes a law, it follows the process described in the Constitution. Each time Americans elect a president, they are following the Constitution's guidelines. Supreme Court justices still settle disagreements over federal laws according to the Constitution.

One of the reasons the Constitution still works so well is that it is flexible. The document focuses on basic rights and principles rather than specific laws. That means modern issues can be solved with the old document. For example, the writers of the Constitution did not know what the Internet was. However, free speech guaranteed in the First Amendment can still be applied to articles published on the Internet.

The Constitution also has remained useful because it can change with the nation. As the country grew and became older, new issues arose. When the Constitution was written, for example, slavery was practiced in the United States. After the US Civil War, the 13th Amendment ended slavery. The ability to amend the

Slavery wasn't officially abolished until the 13th Amendment was ratified after the Civil War.

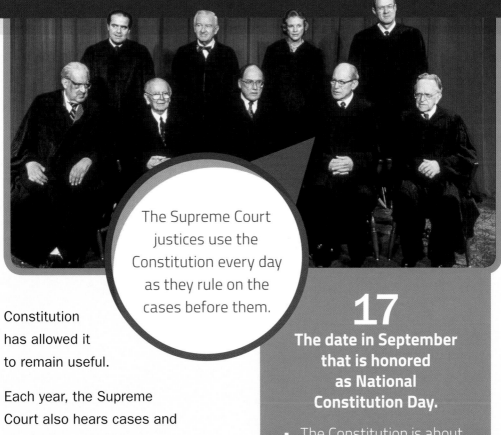

The Supreme Court justices use the Constitution every day as they rule on the cases before them.

Constitution has allowed it to remain useful.

Each year, the Supreme Court also hears cases and determines whether the laws of the Constitution have been followed. In 2014, for example, the Court heard the case *United States v. California*. The case centered on who owned the natural resources in the land that lies under the Pacific Ocean along California's coast. Because it was a disagreement between the United States and a state, it was something the Supreme Court could handle under the Constitution.

The wisdom of the writers of the Constitution lives on today. It has provided a solid foundation for the country as it grew from 13 states

17

The date in September that is honored as National Constitution Day.

- The Constitution is about basic principles rather than specific laws.
- Careful, thoughtful changes to the Constitution have kept it useful for more than 200 years.
- When the Supreme Court decides a case, it still uses the Constitution as its guide.

to 50. The writers' ideas about government and personal rights have shaped the ideas that are part of everyday American lives.

27

Fact Sheet

- The Magna Carta inspired the US Constitution and the Bill of Rights. English noblemen wrote it in 1215 to protect their rights and property from the powerful King John.

- After the American Revolution, many Americans were in debt. State governments refused to forgive the debt and began repossessing debtors' land. In protest, a former soldier named Daniel Shays led a rebellion. It showed how weak the national government was and forced leaders to revise the Articles of Confederation quickly.

- At the Convention, northern and southern states disagreed about how to calculate a state's population. Southerners wanted to count their large slave population, which would allow them more representatives in the government. Many northerners disagreed with this idea. The two groups compromised and counted three-fifths of the total number of slaves in the state's total population.

- The Constitutional Convention took place at the Pennsylvania State House. This is also where the Declaration of Independence was signed and where George Washington was named Commander of the Continental Army. Today, this building is known as Independence Hall.

- The first chance Americans had to read the Constitution was on September 19, 1787. On that day, the full text of the document was printed in a newspaper called *The Pennsylvania Packet and Daily Advertiser*.

- George Washington established the first Thanksgiving Day on November 26, 1789. It was originally meant as a day to give thanks for the US Constitution.

Glossary

abolish
To formally bring an end to a practice or system.

appeal
A request to bring a legal case from a low court to a higher court.

delegate
A person who has been chosen to represent others.

federal
Having to do with a central authority that governs a nation made up of several states.

interpret
To explain the meaning of something, such as a law.

ratify
To approve something officially.

right
A legal claim to something, such as voting or speaking freely.

unanimously
Without disagreement.

veto
The president's right to reject a bill before it becomes a law.

welfare
The health, happiness, and fortunes of a person or group.

For More Information

Books

Friedman, Mark. *The Democratic Process*. New York: Children's Press, 2012.

Steinkraus, Kyla. *Constitution*. Vero Beach, FL: Rourke Educational Media, 2015.

Winter, Jonah. *The Founding Fathers! Those Horse-Ridin', Fiddle-Playin', Book-Readin', Gun-Totin' Gentlemen Who Started America*. New York: Atheneum Books for Young Readers, 2015.

Index

amendments, 15, 21, 22–23, 24, 26
Anti-Federalists, 12–13
Articles of Confederation, 6–7, 8

Bill of Rights, 13, 24–25

Civil War (US), 26
Connecticut Compromise, 8–9
Constitutional Convention, 4, 8–9, 24

Declaration of Independence, 9

executive branch, 9, 14, 18–19

Federalists, 12–13

Hamilton, Alexander, 13

Jay, John, 13
judicial branch, 9, 14, 20–21

legislative branch, 8–9, 14, 16–17, 18, 19, 20–21, 22

Madison, James, 11, 13
Morris, Gouverneur, 10–11

Philadelphia, Pennsylvania, 4, 8
preamble, 10, 14

separation of powers, 5, 9, 14
Shallus, Jacob, 11
Sherman, Roger, 8–9
Supreme Court, 5, 9, 18, 20–21, 26, 27

Washington, George, 9

About the Author

Kate Conley is the author and editor of many children's books. She lives in Minnetonka, Minnesota, with her husband and two children. When she's not writing, she spends her time reading, sewing, and playing with her kids.

READ MORE FROM 12-STORY LIBRARY

Every 12-Story Library book is available in many formats. For more information, visit 12StoryLibrary.com.